To crochet, you need only a crochet hook, some yarn and a tapestry needle.

Yarn

Yarn comes in many sizes: from fine crochet cotton used for doilies, to wonderful bulky mohairs used for afghans and sweaters. The most commonly used yarn is a medium size, called worsted weight (sometimes called 4-ply). It is readily available in a wide variety of beautiful colors. This is the weight we will use in our lessons. Always read yarn labels carefully. The label will tell you how much yarn is in the skein or ball, in ounces, grams or yards; the type of yarn, its washability, and sometimes how to pull the yarn from the skein. Also, there is usually a dye lot number. This number assures you that the color of each skein with this number is the same. The same color may vary from dye lot to dye lot creating variations in color when a project is completed. Therefore, when purchasing yarn for a project, it is important to match the dye lot number on the skeins.

You'll need a blunt-pointed sewing needle with an eye big enough to carry the yarn for weaving in yarn ends and sewing seams. This is a size 16 steel tapestry needle. You can buy big plastic needles called yarn needles, but they are not as good as the steel.

Hooks

Crochet hooks, too, come in many sizes, from very fine steel hooks used to make intricate doilies and lace, to great big fat ones of plastic or wood used to make bulky sweaters or rugs.

The hooks you will use most often are made of aluminum, are about 6" long, and are sized alphabetically by letter from B (the smallest) to K. For our lessons, you'll need a size H hook, a medium size.

The aluminum crochet hook looks like this:

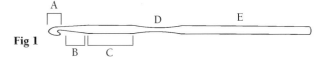

Fig 1

In **Fig 1**, (A) is the hook end, which is used to hook the yarn and draw it through other loops of yarn (called stitches). (B) is the throat, a shaped area that helps you slide the stitch up onto (C) the working area. (D) is the fingerhold, a flattened area that helps you grip the hook comfortably, usually with your thumb and third finger; and (E) is the handle, which rests under your fourth and little fingers, and provides balance for easy, smooth work.

It is important that every stitch is made on the working area, never on the throat (which would make the stitch too tight) and never on the fingergrip (which would stretch the stitch).

The hook is held in the right hand, with the thumb and third finger on the fingergrip, and the index finger near the tip of the hook (**Fig 2**).

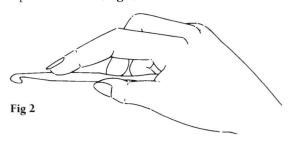

Fig 2

The hook should be turned slightly toward you, not facing up or down. **Fig 3** shows how the hook is held, viewing from underneath the hand. The hook should be held firmly, but not tightly.

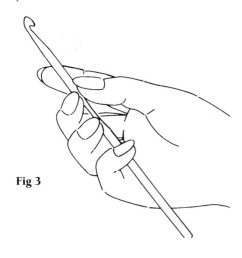

Fig 3

Lesson 2: Chain Stitch (abbreviated ch)

Crochet usually begins with a series of chain stitches called a beginning or starting chain. Begin by making a slip knot on the hook about 6" from the yarn end. Loop the yarn as in **Fig 4**.

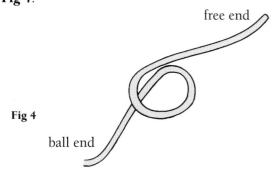

free end

ball end

Fig 4

Insert hook through center of loop and hook the free end (**Fig 5**).

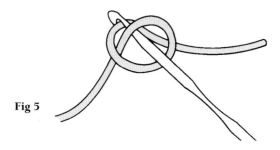

Fig 5

Pull this through and up onto the working area of the hook (**Fig 6**).

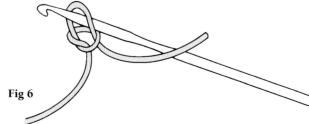

Fig 6

Pull yarn end to tighten the loop (**Fig 7**).

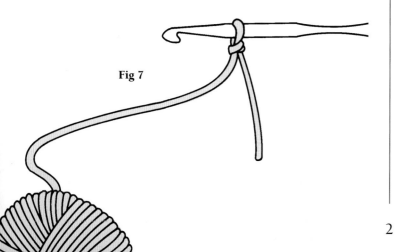

Fig 7

It should be firm, but loose enough to slide back and forth easily on the hook. Be sure you still have about a 6" yarn end.

Hold the hook, now with its slip knot, in your right hand (**Fig 8**).

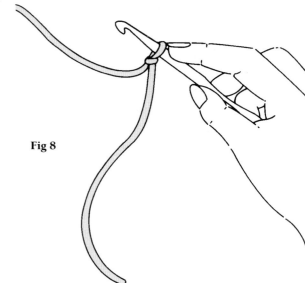

Fig 8

Now let's make the first chain stitch.

Step 1: Hold the base of the slip knot with the thumb and index finger of your left hand, and thread yarn from the skein over the middle finger (**Fig 9**)

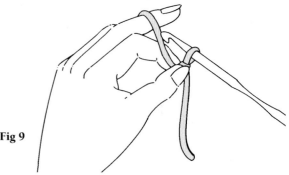

Fig 9

and under the remaining fingers of the left hand (**Fig 9a**).

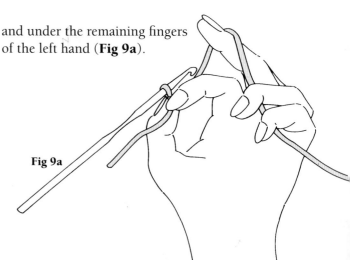

Fig 9a

Your middle finger will stick up a bit to help the yarn feed smoothly from the skein; the other fingers help maintain even tension on the yarn as you work.

Hint: As you practice, you can adjust the way your left hand holds the yarn to whatever is most comfortable for you.

Step 2: Bring the yarn over the hook from back to front and hook it (**Fig 10**).

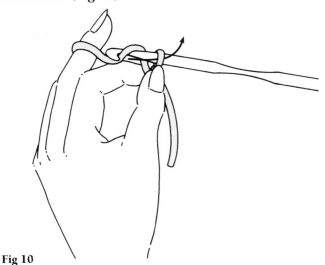

Fig 10

Draw hooked yarn through the loop of the slip knot on the hook and up onto the working area of the hook (see arrow on **Fig 10**); you have now made one chain stitch (**Fig 11**).

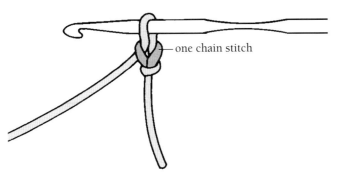

one chain stitch

Step 3: Again bring the yarn over the hook from back to front (**Fig 12**).

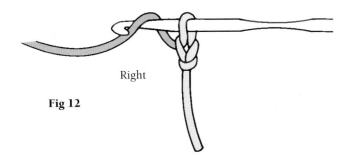

Right

Fig 12

Note: Take care not to bring yarn from front to back (**Fig 12a**).

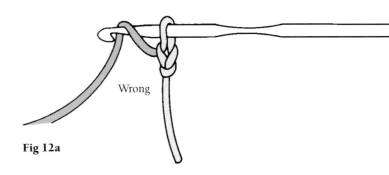

Wrong

Fig 12a

Hook it and draw through loop on the hook: you have made another chain stitch (**Fig 13**).

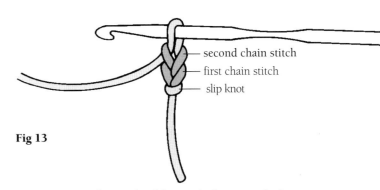

second chain stitch
first chain stitch
slip knot

Fig 13

Repeat Step 3 for each additional chain stitch, being careful to move the left thumb and index finger up the chain close to the hook after each new stitch or two (**Fig 14**). This helps you control the work. Also be sure to pull each new stitch up onto the working area of the hook.

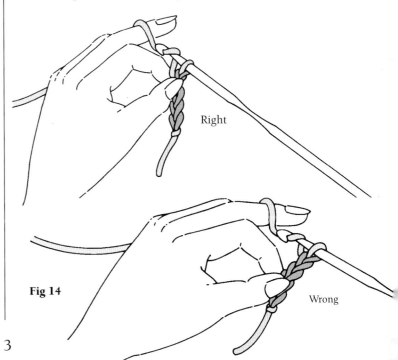

Right

Fig 14

Wrong

The working yarn and the work in progress are always held in your left hand.

Practice making chains until you are comfortable with your grip of the hook and the flow of the yarn; in the beginning your work will be uneven, with some chain stitches loose and others tight. While you're learning, try to keep the chain stitches loose. As your skill increases, the chain should be firm, but not tight, with all chain stitches even in size.

Hint: As you practice, if the hook slips out of a stitch, don't get upset! Just insert the hook again from the front into the center of the last stitch, taking care not to twist the loop (**Fig 15**).

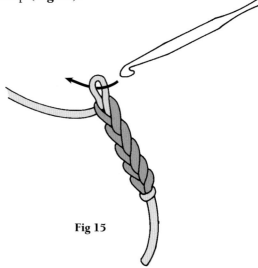

Fig 15

When you are comfortable with the chain stitch, draw your hook out of the last stitch, and pull out the work back to the beginning. Now you've learned the important first step of crochet: the beginning chain.

Lesson 3: Working into the Chain

Once you have worked the starting chain, you are ready to begin the stitches required to make any project. These stitches are worked into the starting chain. For practice, make 6 chains loosely.

Hint: When counting your chain stitches at the start of a pattern – which you must do very carefully before continuing – note that the loop on the hook is never counted as a stitch; and the starting slip knot is never counted as a stitch (**Fig 16**).

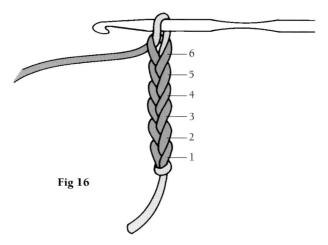

Fig 16

Now stop and look at the chain. The front looks like a series of interlocking V's (**Fig 16**), and each stitch has a bump or ridge at the back (**Fig 17**).

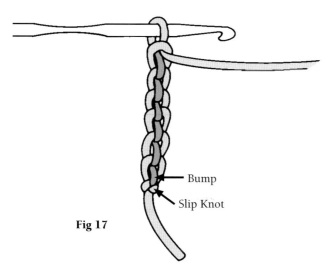

Bump
Slip Knot

Fig 17

You will never work into the first chain from the hook. Depending on the stitch, you will work into the second, third, fourth, etc. chain from the hook. The instructions will always state how many chains to skip before starting the first stitch.

When working a stitch, insert hook from the front of the chain, through the center of a V stitch, and under the corresponding bump on the back of the same stitch (**Fig 18**).

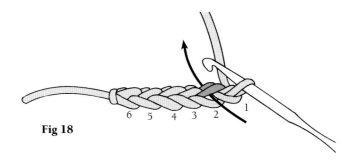

6 5 4 3 2 1

Fig 18

Excluding the first stitch, you will work into every stitch in the chain unless the pattern states differently, but not into the starting slip knot (**Fig 18a**). Be sure that you do not skip that last chain at the end.

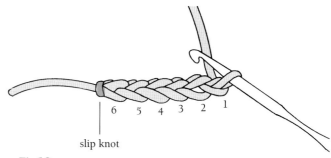

6 5 4 3 2 1

slip knot

Fig 18a

5

Lesson 4: Single Crochet (abbreviated sc)

Most crochet is made with variations of just four different stitches: single crochet, double crochet, half double crochet, and triple crochet. The stitches differ mainly in height, which is varied by the number of times the yarn is wrapped around the hook. The shortest and most basic of these stitches is the single crochet.

Working Row 1

To practice, begin with the chain of 6 stitches made in Lesson 3 and work the first row of single crochet as follows:

Step 1: Skip first chain stitch from hook. Insert hook in the 2nd chain stitch through the center of the V and under the back bump; with third finger of your left hand, bring yarn over the hook from back to front, and hook the yarn (**Fig 19**).

Fig 19

Draw yarn through the chain stitch and well up onto the working area of the hook. You now have 2 loops on the hook (**Fig 20**).

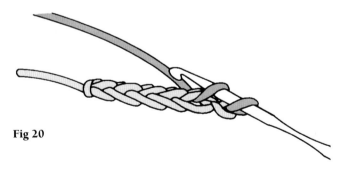

Fig 20

Step 2: Again bring yarn over the hook from back to front, hook it and draw it through both loops on the hook (**Fig 21**).

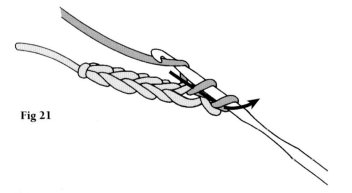

Fig 21

One loop will remain on the hook, and you have made one single crochet (**Fig 22**).

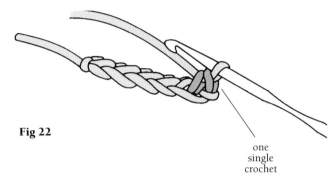

Fig 22

one single crochet

Step 3: Insert hook in next chain stitch as before, hook the yarn, and draw it through the chain stitch; hook yarn again and draw it through both loops: you have made another single crochet.

Repeat Step 3 in each remaining chain stitch, taking care to work in the last chain stitch, **but not in the slip knot.** You have completed one row of single crochet, and should have 5 stitches in the row. **Fig 23** shows how to count the stitches.

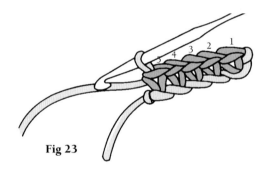

Fig 23

Hint: As you work, be careful not to twist the chain; keep all the V's facing you.

Working Row 2

To work the second row of single crochet, you need to bring the yarn up to the correct height to work the first stitch, and then turn the work so you can work back across the first row. So to raise the yarn, chain 1 (this is called a turning chain), and then turn the work in the direction of the arrow (counterclockwise) as shown in **Fig 24**.

Fig 24

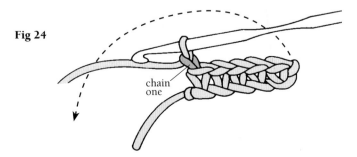

chain one

6

Do not remove the hook from the loop as you do this (**Fig 24a**).

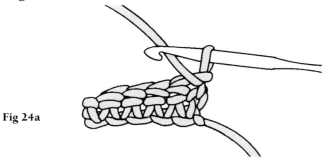

Fig 24a

This row, and all the following rows of single crochet, will be worked into a previous row of single crochet, not into the beginning chain as you did before. Remember that when you worked into the starting chain, you inserted the hook through the center of the V, and under the bump. This is only done when working into a starting chain.

To work into a previous row of crochet, insert the hook under both loops of the previous stitch, as shown in Fig 25, instead of through the center of the V.

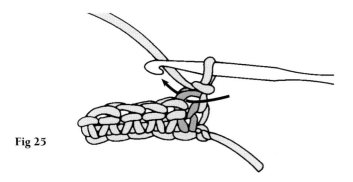

Fig 25

The first single crochet of the row is worked in the last stitch of the previous row (**Fig 25**), not into the turning chain. Work a single crochet in each single crochet to the end, taking care to work in each stitch, especially the last stitch, which is easy to miss (**Fig 26**).

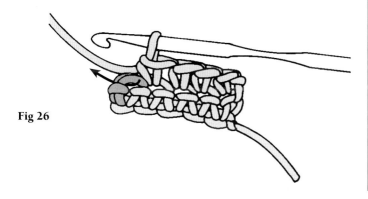

Fig 26

Stop now and count your stitches; you should still have 5 single crochets on the row (**Fig 27**).

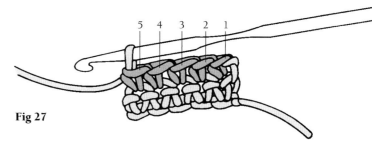

Fig 27

Hint: When you want to pause to count stitches, check your work, have a snack or chat on the phone, you can remove your hook from the work -- but do this at the end of a row, not in the middle. To remove the hook, pull straight up on the hook to make a long loop (**Fig 28**).

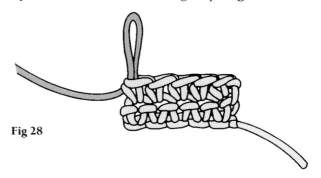

Fig 28

Then withdraw the hook and put it on a table or other safe place (sofas and chairs have a habit of eating crochet hooks). Put work in a safe place so loop is not pulled out. To begin work again, just insert the hook in the big loop (don't twist the loop), and pull on the yarn from the skein to tighten the loop.

To end Row 2, after the last single crochet, chain 1 for the turning chain, and turn the work counterclockwise.

Here is the way instructions for Row 2 might be written in a pattern:

Row 2: Sc in each sc; ch 1, turn.

Note: To save space, a number of abbreviations are used. For a list of abbreviations used in patterns, see page 21.

Working Row 3

Row 3 is worked exactly as you worked Row 2. Here are the instructions as they would be given in a pattern:

Row 3: Rep Row 2.

Now wasn't that easy? For practice, work three more rows, which means you will repeat Row 2 three times more.

Hint: Try to keep your stitches as smooth and even as possible; remember to work loosely rather than tightly, and to make each stitch well up on the working area of the hook. Be sure to chain 1 and turn at the end of each row, and to check carefully to be sure you've worked into the last stitch of each row.

Count the stitches at the end of each row; do you still have 5? Good work.

Hint: What if you don't have 5 stitches at the end of a row? Perhaps you worked two stitches in one stitch, or skipped a stitch. Find your mistake, then just pull out your stitches back to the mistake; pulling out in crochet is simple. Just take out the hook, and gently pull on the yarn. The stitches will come out easily; when you reach the place where you want to start again, insert the hook in the last loop (taking care not to twist it) and begin.

Finishing Off

It's time to move on to another stitch, so let's finish off your single crochet practice piece, which you can keep for future reference. After the last stitch of the last row, cut the yarn, leaving a 6" end. As you did when you took your hook out for a break, draw the hook straight up, but this time draw the yarn cut end completely through the stitch. Photo A shows an actual sample of six rows of single crochet to which you can compare your practice rows and shows how to count the stitches and rows.

Now you can put the piece away, and it won't pull out (you might want to tag this piece as a sample of single crochet).

Photo

Lesson 5: Double Crochet (abbreviated dc)

Double crochet is a taller stitch than single crochet. To practice, first chain 14 stitches loosely. Then work the first row of double crochet as follows:

Working Row 1

Step 1: Bring yarn once over the hook from back to front (as though you were going to make another chain stitch); skip the first three chains from the hook, then insert hook in the 4th chain (**Fig 29**).

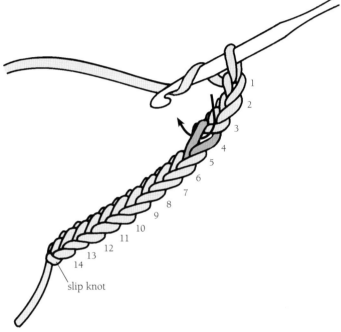

Fig 29

Remember not to count the loop on the hook as a chain. Be sure to go through the center of the V of the chain, and under the bump at the back, and to not twist the chain.

Step 2: Hook yarn and draw it through the chain stitch and up onto the working area of the hook: you now have 3 loops on the hook (**Fig 30**).

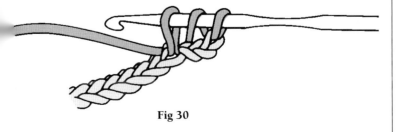

Fig 30

Step 3: Hook yarn and draw through the first 2 loops on the hook (**Fig 31**).

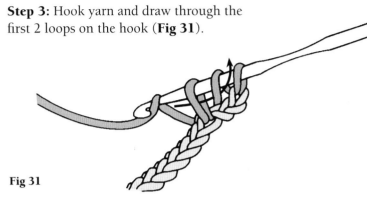

Fig 31

You now have 2 loops on the hook (**Fig 32**).

Fig 32

Step 4: Hook yarn and draw through both loops on the hook (**Fig 33**).

Fig 33

You have now completed one double crochet and one loop remains on the hook (**Fig 34**).

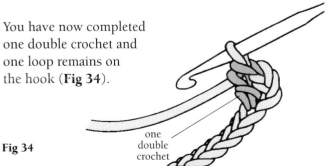

Fig 34

one double crochet

Repeat Steps 1 through 4 in each chain stitch across (except in Step 1, work in next chain, don't skip 3 chains).

When you've worked a double crochet in the last chain, pull out your hook and look at your work, then count your double crochet stitches: there should be 12 of them, counting the first 3 chain stitches you skipped at the beginning of the row as a double crochet (**Fig 35**).

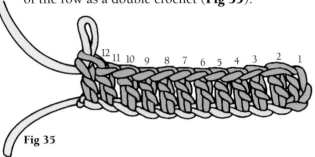

Fig 35

Hint: In working double crochet on a beginning chain row, the 3 chains skipped before making the first double crochet are always counted as a double crochet stitch.

You need to bring the yarn up to the correct height for the next row, and then turn the work. So to raise the yarn, chain 3 (this is called the turning chain); then turn the work counterclockwise before beginning Row 2.

Working Row 2

The 3 chains in the turning chain just made count as the first double crochet of the new row, so skip the first double crochet and work a double crochet in the 2nd stitch (being sure to insert hook under top 2 loops of stitch): **Fig 36** indicates the right and wrong placement of this stitch.

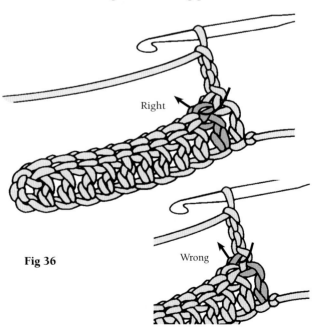

Right

Fig 36   Wrong

Work a double crochet in each remaining stitch across previous row, and be sure at the end of the row to work the last double crochet in the top of the turning chain from the previous row. Be sure to insert hook in the center of the V (and back bump) of the top chain of the turning chain (**Fig 37**). Stop and count your double crochets; there should be 12 stitches. Now, chain 3 and turn.

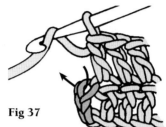

Fig 37

Here is the way the instructions might be written in a pattern:

Row 2: Dc in each dc: you should have 12 dc; ch 3, turn.

Working Row 3

Row 3 is worked exactly as you worked Row 2.

In a pattern, instructions would read:

Row 3: Rep Row 2.

For practice, work 3 more rows, repeating Row 2. At the end of the last row, finish off the piece as you did for the single crochet practice piece. Photo B shows a sample of 6 rows of double crochet and how to count the stitches and rows.

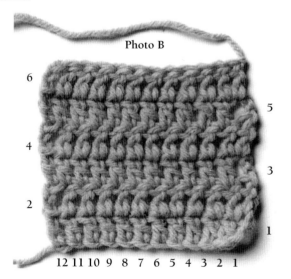

Photo B

Break Time!

Now you have learned the two most often used stitches in crochet. Since you've worked so hard, it's time to take a break. Walk around, relax your hands, have a snack, or just take a few minutes to release the stress that sometimes develops when learning something new.

10

Lesson 6: Half Double Crochet (abbreviated hdc)

Just as its name implies, this stitch eliminates one step of double crochet, and works up about half as tall.

To practice, chain 13 stitches loosely.

Working Row 1

Step 1: Bring yarn once over hook from back to front, skip the first 2 chains, then insert hook in the third chain from the hook (**Fig 38**).

Remember not to count the loop on the hook as a chain.

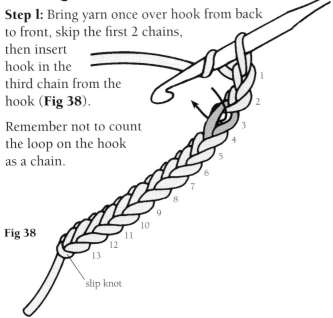

Fig 38

slip knot

Step 2: Hook yarn and draw it through the chain stitch and up onto the working area of the hook. You now have 3 loops on the hook (**Fig 39**).

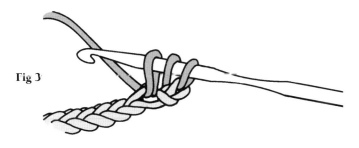

Fig 3

Step 3: Hook yarn and draw it through all 3 loops on the hook in one motion (**Fig 40**).

Fig 40

You have completed one half double crochet and one loop remains on the hook (**Fig 41**).

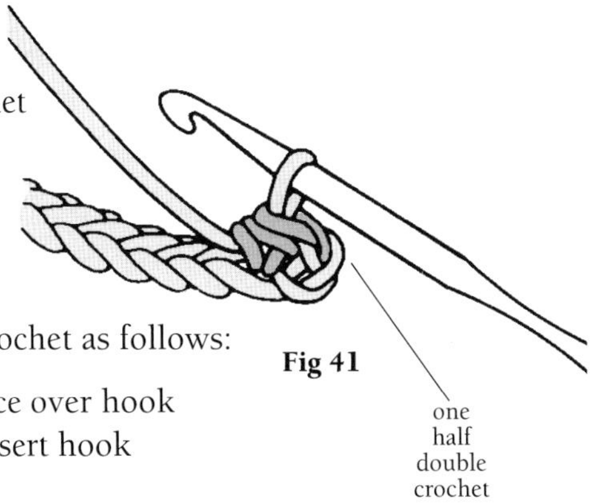

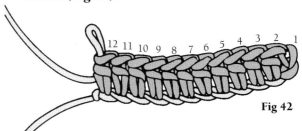

Fig 41

one half double crochet

In next chain stitch work a half double crochet as follows:

Step 1: Bring yarn once over hook from back to front, insert hook in next chain.

Repeat Steps 2 and 3 of Row 1.

Repeat the previous 3 steps in each remaining chain stitch across. Stop and count your stitches; you should have 12 half double crochets, counting the first 2 chains you skipped at the beginning of the row as a half double crochet (**Fig 42**).

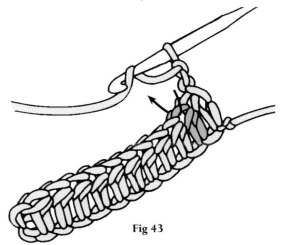

Fig 42

Chain 2 and turn.

Working Row 2

Like double crochet, the turning chain does count as a stitch in half double crochet (unless your pattern specifies otherwise.) Skip the first half double crochet of the previous row and work a half double crochet in the second stitch (**Fig 43**) and in each remaining stitch across the previous row. At the end of the row, chain 2 and turn.

Fig 43

Here is the way the instructions might be written in a pattern:

Row 2: Hdc in each hdc: you should have 12 hdc; ch 2, turn.

Working Row 3

Row 3 is worked exactly as you worked Row 2.

For practice, work 3 more rows, repeating Row 2. Be sure to count your stitches carefully at the end of each row. When the practice rows are completed, finish off. Photo C shows a sample of 6 rows of half double crochet and how to count the stitches and the rows. Continue with the next lesson.

Photo C

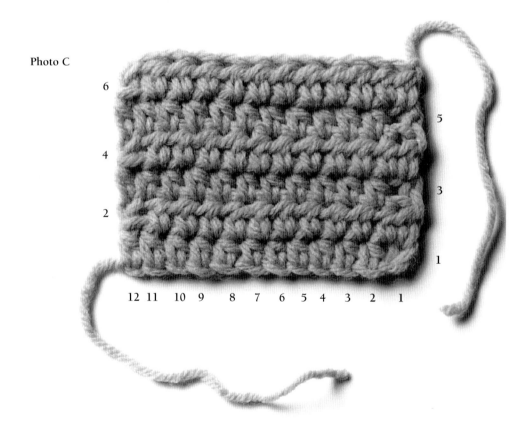

12

Lesson 7: Triple Crochet (abbreviated trc)

Triple crochet is a tall stitch that works up quickly and is fun to do. Sometimes in instructions it is called treble crochet. To practice, first chain 15 stitches loosely. Then work the first row as follows:

Working Row 1

Step 1: Bring yarn twice over the hook (from back to front), skip the first four chains, then insert hook into the 5th chain from the hook (**Fig 44**).

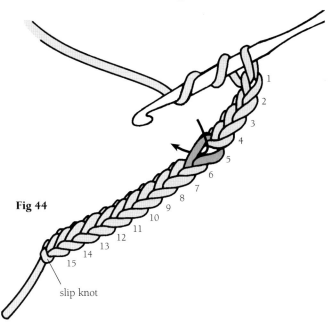

Fig 44

slip knot

Step 2: Hook yarn and draw it through the chain stitch and up onto the working area of the hook; you now have 4 loops on the hook (**Fig 45**).

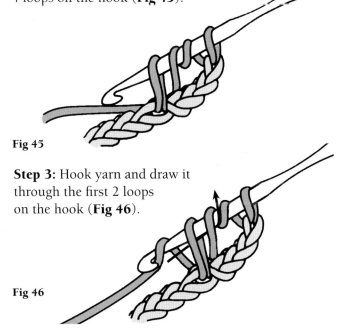

Fig 45

Step 3: Hook yarn and draw it through the first 2 loops on the hook (**Fig 46**).

Fig 46

You now have 3 loops on the hook (**Fig 46a**).

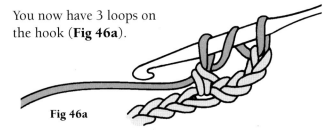

Fig 46a

Step 4: Hook yarn again and draw it through the next 2 loops on the hook (**Fig 47**).

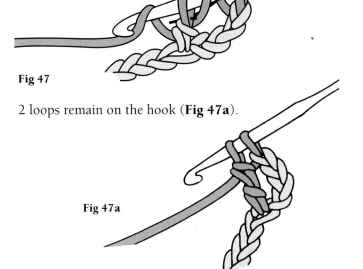

Fig 47

2 loops remain on the hook (**Fig 47a**).

Fig 47a

Step 5: Hook yarn and draw it through both remaining loops on the hook (**Fig 48**).

Fig 48

You have now completed one triple crochet and one loop remains on the hook (**Fig 49**).

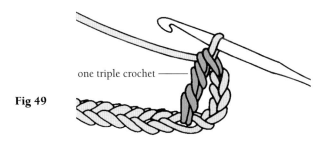

one triple crochet

Fig 49

In next chain stitch work a triple crochet as follows:

Step 1: Bring yarn twice over the hook (from back to front), insert hook in the next chain (**Fig 50**).

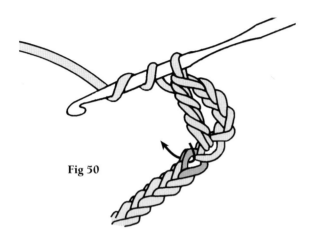

Fig 50

Steps 2 through 5: Repeat the preceding Steps 2 through 5.

Repeat the previous 5 steps in each remaining chain stitch across.

When you've worked a triple crochet in the last chain, count your stitches: there should be 12 of them, counting the first 4 chains you skipped at the beginning of the row as a triple crochet (**Fig 51**); chain 4 and turn.

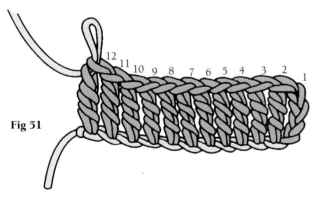

Fig 51

Hint: In working the first row of triple crochet, the 4 chains skipped before making the first triple crochet are always counted as a triple crochet stitch.

Working Row 2

The 4 turning chains have brought your yarn up to the correct height, and count as the first stitch of the row. So skip the first stitch, and work a triple crochet in the second stitch (**Fig 52**).

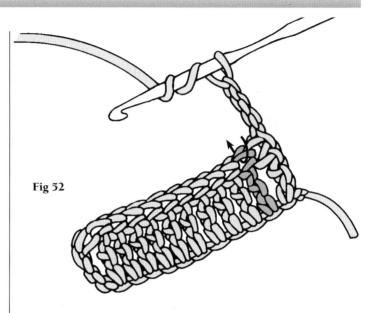

Fig 52

Work a triple crochet in each remaining stitch across previous row, being sure at end to work last triple crochet in the top of the turning chain from the previous row. Count stitches; be sure you still have 12 stitches; chain 4 and turn.

Hint: Remember to work last trc of each row in turning chain of previous row. Missing this stitch in the turning chain is a common error.

Here is the way the instructions might be written in a pattern:

Row 2: Trc in each trc: you should have 12 trc; ch 4, turn.

Working Row 3

Work Row 3 exactly as you worked Row 2.

For practice, work 3 more rows, repeating Row 2. At the end of the last row, finish off the piece. Photo D shows a sample of 6 rows of triple crochet and how to count the stitches and rows.

Photo D

Lesson 8: Slip Stitch (abbreviated sl st)

This is the shortest of all crochet stitches, and is really more a technique than a stitch. Slip stitches are usually used to move yarn across a group of stitches without adding height, or to join work.

Moving Yarn Across Stitches

Chain 10.

Working Row 1

Double crochet in the 4th chain from hook (see page 9) and in each chain across. On the next row, you are going to slip stitch across the first four stitches before beginning to work double crochet again. So instead of making 3 chains for the turning chain as you would usually do for a second row of double crochet, this time just chain 1 and turn.

Working Row 2

The turning ch-1 does not count as a stitch; therefore insert hook under both loops of first stitch, hook yarn, and draw it through both loops of stitch and loop on the hook (**Fig 53**): one slip stitch made.

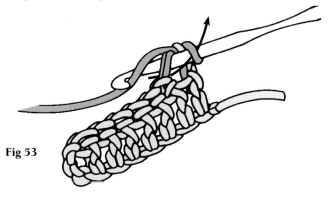

Fig 53

Work a slip stitch in the same manner in each of the next 3 stitches. Now we're going to finish the row in double crochet; chain 3 to get yarn at the right height (the chain 3 counts as a double crochet), then work a double crochet in each of the remaining stitches. Look at your work and see how we moved the yarn across with slip stitches, adding very little height (**Fig 54**).

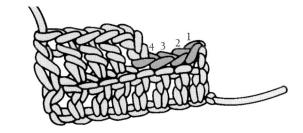

Fig 54

Finish off and save the sample.

Here is the way the instructions might be written in a pattern.

Row 2: Sl st in next 4 dc; ch 3, dc in each rem dc: 5 dc. Finish off.

Hint: When slip stitching across stitches, always work very loosely.

Joining Stitches

Joining a chain into a circle.

Chain 6, then insert hook through the first chain you made (next to the slip knot, **Fig 55**).

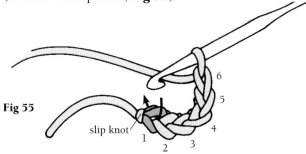

Fig 55

slip knot

Hook yarn and draw it through the chain and through the loop on hook; you have now joined the 6 chains into a circle or ring. This is the way many motifs, such as the granny square, are started. Cut yarn and keep this practice piece as a sample.

Joining the end of a round to the beginning of the same round.

Chain 6; join with a slip stitch in first chain you made to form a ring. Chain 3, work 11 double crochet in ring; insert hook in 3rd chain of beginning chain 3 (**Fig 56**), hook yarn and draw it through the chain and through the loop on the hook; you have how joined the round. Cut yarn and keep this piece as a sample.

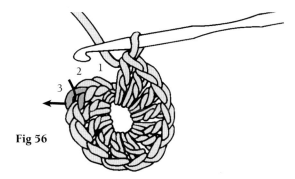

Fig 56

Here is the way the instructions might be written in a pattern:

Rnd 1: Ch 3, 11 dc in ring; join in 3rd ch of beg ch-3.

Lesson 9: Stitch Sampler

You've now learned the basic stitches of crochet – and wasn't it fun? The hard part is over!

To help you understand the difference in the way single crochet, half double crochet, double crochet and triple crochet stitches are worked, and the difference in their heights, let's make one more sample.

Chain 17 stitches loosely. Taking care not to work too tightly, single crochet in the second chain from hook and in each of the next three chains; work a half double crochet in each of the next four chains; work a double crochet in each of the next four chains; work a triple crochet in each of the next four chains; finish off. Your work should look like Photo E.

Now in 9 easy lessons you've become a crocheter! You're ready to start your first project – will it be an afghan, a vest, a baby afghan and hat, potholders, a doll outfit? Be sure to read the following section on Special Helps before you start.

Photo E

Special Helps

Increasing and Decreasing

Shaping is done by increasing, which adds stitches to make the crocheted piece wider; or decreasing, which subtracts stitches to make the piece narrower.

Note: Make a practice sample by chaining 15 loosely and working 4 rows of single crochet with 14 stitches in each row. Do not finish off at end of last row. Use this sample swatch to practice the following method of increasing stitches.

Increasing: To increase one stitch in single, half double, double or triple crochet, simply work two stitches in one stitch. For example, if you are working in single crochet and you need to increase one stitch, you would work one single crochet in the next stitch; then you would work another single crochet in the same stitch.

For practice: On sample swatch, chain 1 and turn. Single crochet in first 2 stitches; increase in next stitch by working 2 single crochets in stitch (**Fig 57**).

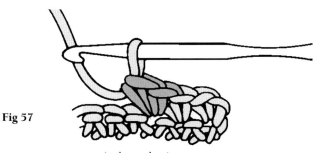

Fig 57

single crochet increase

Repeat increase in each stitch across row to last 2 stitches; single crochet in each of next 2 stitches. Count your stitches; you should have 24 stitches. If you don't have 24 stitches, examine your swatch to see if you have increased in each specified stitch. Rework the row if necessary.

Increases in half double, double and triple crochet are shown in **Fig 57a**.

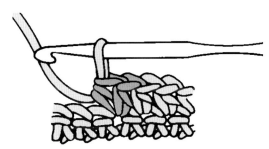

Fig 57a   half double crochet increase

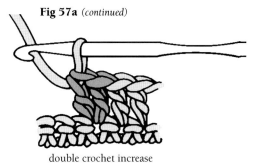

Fig 57a (continued)

double crochet increase

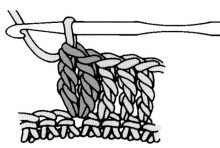

triple crochet increase

Note: Make another practice sample by chaining 15 loosely and working 4 rows of single crochet. Do not finish off at end of last row. Use this sample swatch to practice the following methods of decreasing stitches.

Decreasing: This is how to work a decrease in the four main stitches. Each decrease gives one fewer stitch than you had before.

Single Crochet Decrease: Insert hook and draw up a loop in each of the next 2 stitches (3 loops now on hook), hook yarn and draw through all 3 loops on the hook (**Fig 58**).

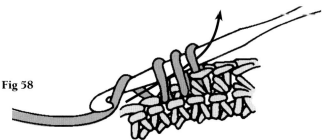

Fig 58

Single crochet decrease made (**Fig 59**).

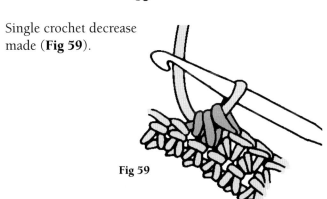

Fig 59

17

Double Crochet Decrease: Work a double crochet in the specified stitch until 2 loops remain on the hook (**Fig 60**).

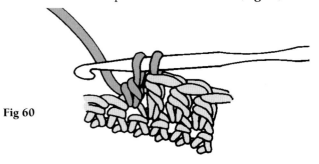

Fig 60

Keeping these 2 loops on hook, work another double crochet in the next stitch until 3 loops remain on hook; hook yarn and draw through all 3 loops on the hook (**Fig 61**).

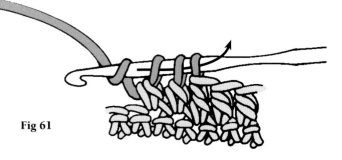

Fig 61

Double crochet decrease made (**Fig 62**).

Fig 62

Half Double Crochet Decrease: YO, insert hook in specified stitch and draw up a loop: 3 loops on the hook (**Fig 63**).

Fig 63

Keeping these 3 loops on hook, YO and draw up a loop in the next stitch (5 loops now on hook), hook yarn and draw through all 5 loops on the hook (**Fig 64**).

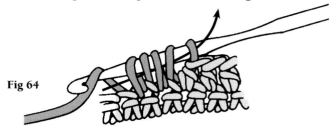

Fig 64

Half double crochet decrease made (**Fig 65**).

Fig 65

Triple Crochet Decrease: Work a triple crochet in the specified stitch until 2 loops remain on the hook (**Fig 66**).

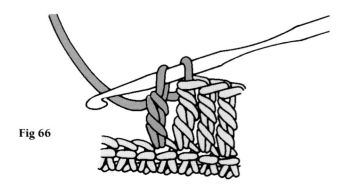

Fig 66

Keeping these 2 loops on hook, work another triple crochet in the next stitch until 3 loops remain on the hook, hook yarn and draw through all 3 loops on the hook (**Fig 67**).

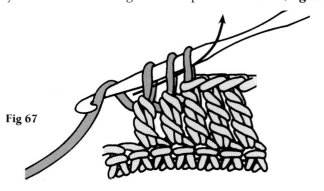

Fig 67

Triple crochet decrease made (**Fig 68**).

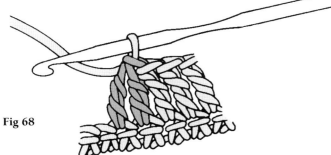

Fig 68

Joining New Yarn

Never tie or leave knots! In crochet, yarn ends can be easily worked in and hidden because of the density of the stitches. Always leave at least 6" ends when finishing off yarn just used and when joining new yarn. If a flaw or a knot appears in the yarn while you are working from a ball or skein, cut out the imperfection and rejoin the yarn.

Whenever possible, join new yarn at the end of a row. To do this, work the last stitch with the old yarn until 2 loops remain on the hook, then with the new yarn complete the stitch (**Fig 69**).

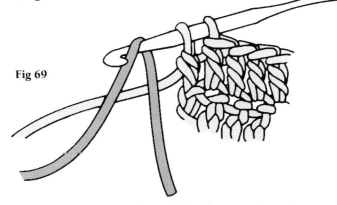

Fig 69

To join new yarn in the middle of a row, when about 12" of the old yarn remain, work several more stitches with the old yarn, working the stitches over the end of new yarn (**Fig 70** shown in double crochet). Then change yarns in stitch as previously explained.

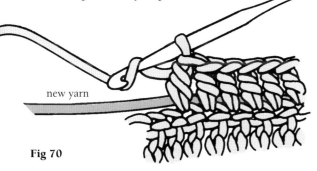

new yarn

Fig 70

Continuing with the new yarn, work the following stitches over the old yarn end.

Finishing

A carefully crocheted project can be disappointing if the finishing has been done incorrectly. Correct finishing techniques are not difficult, but do require time, attention, and a knowledge of basic techniques.

Weaving in Ends: The first procedure of finishing is to securely weave in all yarn ends. Thread a size 16 steel tapestry needle with yarn, then weave running stitches either horizontally or vertically on the wrong side of work. First weave about 2" in one direction and then 1" in the reverse direction. Be sure yarn doesn't show on right side of work. Cut off excess yarn. Never weave in more than one yarn end at a time.

Sewing Seams: Edges in crochet are usually butted together for seaming instead of layered, to avoid bulk. Do not sew too tightly–seams should be elastic and have the same stretch as the crocheted pieces.

Carefully matching stitches and rows as much as possible, sew the seams with the same yarn you used when crocheting.

1. Invisible Seam: This seam provides a smooth, neat appearance as the edges are woven together invisibly from the right side. Join vertical edges, such as side or sleeve seams, through the matching edge stitches, bringing the yarn up through the posts of the stitches (**Fig 71**).

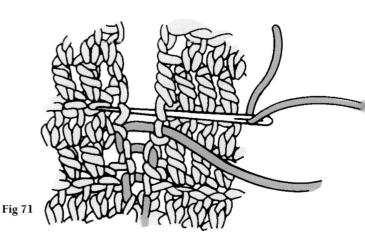

Fig 71

If a firmer seam is desired, weave the edges together through both the tops and the posts of the matching edge stitches.

2. Backstitch Seam: This method gives a strong, firm edge, and is used when the seam will have a lot of stress or pull on it. Hold the pieces with right sides together and then sew through both thicknesses as shown (**Fig 72**).

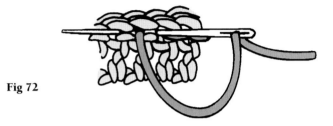

Fig 72

3. Overcast Seam: Strips and pieces of afghans are frequently joined in this manner. Hold the pieces with right sides together and overcast edges, carefully matching stitches on the two pieces (**Fig 73**).

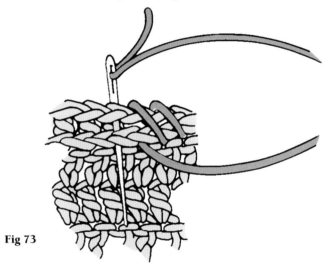

Fig 73

Edges can also be joined in this manner, using only the back loops or the front loops of each stitch (see page 21).

4. Crocheted Seam: Holding pieces with right sides together, join yarn with a slip stitch at right side edge. Loosely slip stitch pieces together, being sure not to pull stitches too tightly (**Fig 74**). You may wish to use a hook one size larger than the one used in the project.

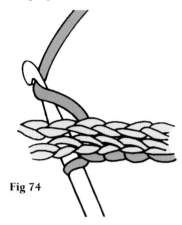

Fig 74

Edging

Single Crochet Edging: A row of single crochet worked around a completed project gives a finished look. The instructions will say to "work a row of single crochet, taking care to keep work flat." This means you need to adjust your stitches as you work. To work the edging, insert hook from front to back through the edge stitch and work a single crochet. Continue evenly along the edge. You may need to skip a row or a stitch here or there to keep the edging from rippling, or add a stitch to keep the work from pulling.

When working around a corner, it is usually necessary to work at least 3 stitches in the corner center stitch to keep the corner flat and square (**Fig 75**).

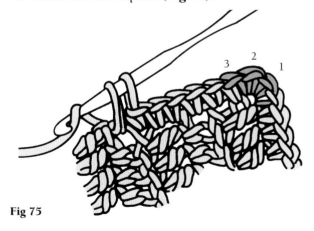

Fig 75

Reading Patterns (abbreviations, symbols and terms)

Crochet patterns are written in a special language full of abbreviations, asterisks, parentheses, and other symbols and terms. These short forms are used so instructions will not take up too much space. They may seem confusing at first, but once understood, they are really easy to follow.

Abbreviations

beg	begin(ning)
bl(s)	back loop(s)
ch(s)	chain(s)
dc	double crochet(s)
dec	decrease(-ing)
Fig	figure
fl(s)	front loop(s)
hdc	half double crochet(s)
inc	increase(-ing)
lp(s)	loops(s)
patt	pattern
prev	previous
rem	remain(ing)
rep	repeat(ing)
rnd(s)	round(s)
sc	single crochet(s)
sk	skip
sl	slip
sl st(s)	slip stitch(es)
sp(s)	space(s)
st(s)	stitch(es)
Tch	turning chain
tog	together
trc	triple crochet(s)
YO	yarn over

Symbols

* An asterisk is used to mark the beginning of a portion of instructions which will be worked more than once; thus, "rep from * twice" means after working the instructions once, repeat the instructions following the asterisk twice more (3 times in all).

† The dagger identifies a portion of instructions that will be repeated again later in the same row or round.

: The number after the colon at the end of a row or round indicates the number of stitches you should have when the row or round has been completed.

( ) Parentheses are used to enclose instructions which should be worked the exact number of times specified immediately following the parentheses, such as: (ch 3, dc) twice. They are also used to set off and clarify a group of stitches that are to be worked all into the same space or stitch, such as: in corner sp work (2 dc, ch 1, 2 dc).

[ ] Brackets and ( ) parentheses are used to provide additional information to clarify instructions.

Terms

Front loop is the loop toward you at the top of the stitch (**Fig 76**).

Back loop is the loop away from you at the top of the stitch (**Fig 76**).

Post is the vertical part of the stitch (**Fig 76**).

Work even means to continue to work in the pattern as established, without increasing or decreasing.

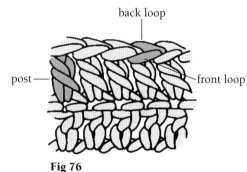

Fig 76

Wrong Side: Wrong side of the work– the side that will not show when project is in use.

Right Side: The side that will show.

Right-hand Side: The side nearest your right hand as you are working.

Left-hand Side: The side nearest your left hand as you are working.

Right Front: The piece of a garment that will be worn on the right-hand side of the body.

Left Front: The piece of a garment that will be worn on the left-hand side of the body.

Gauge

We've left this until last, but it really is the single most important thing in crochet.

If you don't work to gauge, your crocheted garments may not fit correctly, and you may not have enough yarn to finish your project.

Gauge means the number of stitches per inch and rows per inch, that result from a specified yarn worked with a specified size hook. Since everyone crochets differently–some loosely, some tightly, some in between–the measurements of individual work can vary greatly when using the same size hook and yarn. It is **your responsibility** to make sure you achieve the gauge specified in the pattern.

Hook sizes given in instructions are merely guides and should never be used without making a 4" square sample swatch to check gauge. Make the sample gauge swatch using the size hook and the yarn and stitch specified in the pattern. If you have more stitches per inch than specified, try again using a larger size hook. If you have fewer stitches per inch than specified, try again using a smaller size hook. Do not hesitate to change to a larger or smaller size hook if necessary to achieve gauge.

If you have the correct number of stitches per inch, but cannot achieve the row gauge, adjust the height of your stitches. This means that after inserting the hook to begin a new stitch, draw up a little more yarn if your stitches are not tall enough–this makes the first loop slightly higher; or draw up less yarn if your stitches are too tall. Practice will help you achieve the correct height.

Photo F shows how to measure your gauge.

Photo F

Easy Crochet Projects

1: Vest

This Vest is crocheted side to side in three pieces using single and double crochet stitches.

Size:

Small (34 - 36), medium (38), and large (40 - 42)
Finished chest measurements: About 38" (42", 46")
Instructions are written for size small (sm). Changes for sizes medium (med) and large (lg) are in parentheses ( ).

Materials:

Sport weight yarn,
    10 1/2 oz (1155 yds) brushed acrylic or mohair-type,
    brown
Size F aluminum crochet hook, or size required for gauge
Size 16 yarn or tapestry needle
Two 7/8" buttons (optional)

Gauge:

4 sc = 1"

Instructions

Left Side

Ch 146 (150, 154) loosely.

Row 1: Sc in 2nd ch from hook and in each rem ch: 145 (149, 153) sc; ch 1, turn.

Row 2: Sc in each sc; ch 1, turn.

Row 3: Sc in each sc; ch 4 (counts as a dc and a ch-1 on following row), turn.

Row 4: * Dc in next sc, ch 1, sk next sc; rep from * across to last sc; dc in last sc; ch 1, turn.

Row 5: Sc in each dc and in each ch; ch 1, turn.

Rep Rows 2 through 5 in sequence until side measures about 9 1/2" (10 1/2", 11 1/2") from beg.

Rep Row 2 once more; finish off.

Right Side

Work same as for Left Side.

Ribbing

Ch 13.

Row 1: Sc in 2nd ch from hook and in each rem ch: 12 sc; ch 1, turn.

Row 2: Sc in bl (see page 21) of each sc; ch 1, turn.

Rep Row 2 until ribbing measures 36" (40", 44") when slightly stretched.

Finishing

Place Left and Right Sides with right sides facing you and center backs together. Sew edges together using overcast st (see page 20), beginning at lower center back, about 18" (18 1/2", 19") to back of neck.

Fold in half at shoulders.

Weave side seams from bottom, leaving 9" openings for armholes.

Weave ribbing to body of Vest, beg and ending at center front and easing to fit.

Sew ends of ribbing tog at center front.

Attach buttons to ribbing if desired.

2: Country Ripple

designed by Rena V. Stevens

Size:

About 51" x 84"

Materials:

Worsted weight yarn,
23 oz (1610 yds) off white;
15 oz (1050 yds) med blue;
8 oz (560 yds) dk rose;
4 oz (280 yds) rose
Size J aluminum crochet hook, or size required for gauge

Gauge:

3 dc= 1"
4 dc rows = 3"

Instructions

With med blue, ch 157 loosely.

Row 1 (wrong side): Sc in 2nd ch from hook and in each rem ch, changing to rose in last sc (see *Special Helps*, page 19): 156 sc; ch 3 (counts as first dc on following rows), turn.

Row 2 (right side): Dc in next sc, dec over next 2 sts [to work dec: (YO and draw up lp in next st, YO and draw through 2 lps on hook) twice; YO and draw through all 3 lps on hook: dec made]; * dc in next 7 sts, 2 dc in each of next 4 sts; dc in next 7 sts, dec as before 4 times; rep from * 5 times more, ending last rep without working last 2 dec and changing to med blue in last dec; ch 1, turn.

Row 3: Working in fls only, sc in each st, changing to off white in last sc; ch 2 (counts as first hdc on following rows), turn.

Row 4: Sk first sc, * hdc dec over next 2 sc [to work hdc dec: (YO and draw up lp in next st) twice; YO and draw through all 5 lps on hook: hdc dec made]; hdc in next 8 sc, 2 hdc in next sc, hdc in next 2 sc, 2 hdc in next sc, hdc in next 8 sc, hdc dec as before; hdc in next 2 sc; rep from * 5 times more, ending last rep without working last hdc and changing to dk rose in last hdc; ch 1, turn.

Row 5: Working in fls only, sc in each st, changing to med blue in last sc; ch 4 (counts as first trc on following rows), turn.

Row 6: Sk first sc, trc in next sc, trc dec over next 2 sc [to work trc dec: (YO twice, draw up lp in next st, YO and draw through 2 lps on hook, YO and draw through 2 lps on hook) twice; YO and draw through all 3 lps on hook: trc dec made]; * trc in next 7 sts, 2 trc in each of next 4 sts; trc in next 7 sts, trc dec as before 4 times; rep from * 5 times more, ending last rep without working last 2 trc dec and changing to dk rose in last trc dec; ch 1, turn.

Row 7: Rep Row 3.

Row 8: Rep Row 4, changing to med blue in last hdc.

Row 9: Working in fls only, sc in each st, changing to dk rose in last sc; ch 3, turn.

Row 10: Rep Row 2.

Row 11: Working in fls only, sc in each st, changing to off white in last sc; ch 4, turn.

Row 12: Sk first sc, trc in next sc, trc dec; * trc in next 7 sts, 2 trc in each of next 4 sc, trc in next 7 sc, trc dec 4 times; rep from * 5 times more, ending last rep without working last 2 trc dec; ch 3, turn.

Row 13: Working in fls only, sk first trc, dc in next trc, dec; * dc in next 7 sts, 2 dc in each of next 4 sts; dc in next 7 sts, dec 4 times; rep from * 5 times more, ending last rep without working last 2 dec and leaving last st unworked; ch 4, turn.

Row 14: Trc in next dc, trc dec; * trc in next 7 sts, 2 trc in each of next 4 sts; trc in next 7 sts, trc dec 4 times; rep from * 5 times more, ending last rep without working last 2 trc dec and changing to med blue in last trc dec; ch 1, turn.

Row 15: Working in fls only, sc in each st across to last st, changing to lt rose in last sc; leave last st unworked; ch 3, turn.

Rep Rows 2 through 15 seven times.

Rep Rows 2 through 11 once. At end of last row, do not change color or ch 4. Finish off and weave in ends.

3: Doll Dress

Materials:

Worsted weight yarn,
   7 oz (490 yds) pink;
   6 oz (420 yds) off white
Size F aluminum crochet hook, or size required for gauge
13" plastic doll with shoes

Trimmings:

5 yds 3mm fused pink pearls
1 yd 7/8"-wide white satin ribbon
1 yd 1/8"-wide white satin ribbon
4 yds 1/4"-wide pre-gathered white lace
seven 5/8" white ribbon roses
six 3/8" white ribbon roses with pearls
3 snaps, 4/0
sewing needle and matching thread

Gauge:

4 dc = 1"
2 dc rows = 1"

Special Note: Both stitch and row gauge must be accurate in order for dress to fit properly. Bodice is designed to fit snugly.

Instructions

Dress

Bodice:

Starting at neckline with pink, ch 22.

Row 1 (right side): 2 sc in 2nd ch from hook and in each rem ch: 42 sc; ch 2 (counts as first hdc on following rows).

Row 2: Working in fls only, hdc in each sc; ch 1, turn.

Row 3: Sc in each hdc; ch 2, turn.

Row 4: Hdc in next 4 sc; ch 4: underarm section made; sk next 10 sc, hdc in next 12 sc; ch 4: underarm section made; sk next 10 sc, hdc in next 5 sc: 30 sts; ch 1, turn.

Row 5: Sc in each hdc and in each ch; ch 2, turn.

Row 6: Hdc in each sc; ch 1, turn.

Row 7: Sc in each hdc; ch 2, turn.

Row 8: Rep Row 6.

Row 9: Sc in each hdc; ch 3 (counts as first dc on following row), turn.

Row 10: Dc in first sc, 2 dc in each rem sc: 60 dc; ch 3, turn.

Skirt:

Note: Skirt is worked in rnds. Do not turn.

Rnd 1: Working in fls only, dc in first dc, 2 dc in each rem dc; join in 3rd ch of turning ch-3: 120 dc. Change to white by drawing lp through; cut pink.

Rnd 2: Ch 3 (counts as a dc on this and following rnds), working in bls only, dc in each dc; join in 3rd ch of beg ch-3. Change to pink by drawing lp through; cut white.

Rnd 3: Ch 3, working in bls only, dc in each dc; join in 3rd ch of beg ch-3.

Rnd 4: Ch 3, working through both lps, dc in each dc; join in 3rd ch of beg ch-3. Change to white by drawing lp through; cut pink.

Rnds 5 through 10: Rep Rnds 2 through 4 twice.

Rnd 11: Rep Rnd 2.

Skirt Ruffle:

Rnd 12: Ch 3, 2 dc in same ch as joining; working in bls only, 2 dc in next dc; * 3 dc in next dc; 2 dc in next dc; rep from * around; join in 3rd ch of beg ch-3.

Rnd 13: Ch 3, 2 dc in next dc; * dc in next dc, 2 dc in next dc; rep from * around; join in 3rd ch of beg ch-3. Change to white by drawing lp through; cut pink.

Rnd 14: Ch 3, 2 dc in next dc; * dc in next dc, 2 dc in next dc; rep from * around; join in 3rd ch of beg ch-3.

Rnd 15: Ch 1, sc in same ch as joining; * ch 3, sk next dc, sc in next dc; rep from * around, ending last rep without working last sc; join in first sc. Finish off and weave in all ends.

Underskirt:

Hold Dress upside down with right side facing you; fold edge of skirt toward you so unused lps of Row 10 of bodice are at top. Join white in first unused lp of Row 10.

Rnd 1: Ch 3 (counts as a dc on this and following rnds), dc in same lp as joining; 2 dc in each rem lp; join in 3rd ch of beg ch-3: 120 dc.

Rnd 2: Ch 3, dc in each dc; join in 3rd ch of beg ch-3.

Rnds 3 through 10: Rep Rnd 2.

Rnd 11: Ch 3, dc in same ch as joining; 2 dc in each dc; join in 3rd ch of beg ch-3. Finish off and weave in ends.

Sleeve Cap Trim:
Hold Dress with right side facing you; join white in first unused sc of Row 3; ch 1, sc in same sc as joining; * ch 1, sc in next sc; rep from * 8 times more. Finish off and weave in ends.

Work other sleeve cap trim in same manner.

Hat

> **Note:** Hat is worked in rnds. Do not turn; mark beg of rnds.

With pink, ch 5; join to a ring.

Rnd 1 (right side): Ch 1, 8 sc in ring; join in first sc: 8 sc.

Rnd 2: Ch 2 (counts as an hdc on this and following rnds), hdc in same sc as joining; 2 hdc in each rem sc; join in 2nd ch of beg ch-2: 16 hdc.

Rnd 3: Ch 1, 2 sc in same ch as joining; 2 sc in each hdc; join in first sc: 32 sc.

Rnd 4: Ch 2, hdc in same sc as joining; hdc in next sc, * 2 hdc in next sc; hdc in next sc; rep from * around; join in 2nd ch of beg ch-2: 48 hdc.

Rnd 5: Ch 1, sc in same ch as joining; working in bls only, sc in each hdc; join in first sc.

Rnd 6: Ch 2, hdc in each sc; join in 2nd ch of beg ch-2.

Rnd 7: Ch 1, sc in same ch as joining; sc in each hdc; join in fl of first sc.

Rnd 8: Ch 2, working in fls only, hdc in each sc; join in 2nd ch of beg ch-2.

Rnd 9: Ch 1, sc in same ch as joining; 2 sc in next hdc; * sc in next hdc, 2 sc in next hdc; rep from * around; join in first sc: 72 sc.

Rnd 10: Ch 2, hdc in each sc; join in 2nd ch of beg ch-2.

Rnd 11: Rep Rnd 9: 108 sc. At end of rnd, change to white by drawing lp through; cut pink.

Rnd 12: Ch 1, sc in same sc as joining; * ch 3, sk next sc, sc in next sc; rep from * around, ending last rep without working last sc; join in first sc. Finish off and weave in all ends.

Finishing

Step 1: Sew snaps evenly spaced along back opening of Dress.

Step 2: Referring to photo for placement, sew lace along lower edge of each white row of skirt.

Step 3: Sew fused pearls over edge of each row of lace. Referring to photo for placement, sew pearls along Row 2 of Dress bodice. Place Dress on doll.

Step 4: Sew one 5/8" ribbon rose in center of 7/8"-wide white ribbon. Referring to photo for placement, sew three 3/8" ribbon roses around each side of 5/8" ribbon rose. Make a loop with pearls on each side of 5/8" ribbon rose, wrapping pearls around rose; tack in place. Place ribbon around doll's waist and tie bow in back.

Step 5: For Hat, weave 1/8"-wide ribbon through Rnd 6; tie ends in bow at back. Sew lace along Rnd 8; sew pearls along edge of lace. Referring to photo for placement, sew remaining ribbon roses along front of Hat crown.

4: Sunshine and Ruffles

Size:

About 10" diameter

Materials:

Worsted weight yarn,
  50 yds white;
  75 yds yellow
Size G aluminum crochet hook,
  or size required for gauge

Gauge:

4 dc = 1"

Instructions

Front

With yellow, ch 6; join to form a ring.

Rnd 1: Ch 1, 12 sc in ring; join in first sc: 12 sc.

Rnd 2: Ch 1, sc in same sc as joining; 3 dc in next sc; (sc in next sc, 3 dc in next sc) 5 times; join in first sc: six 3-dc groups. Change to white by drawing lp through; cut yellow.

Rnd 3: Ch 3 (counts as a dc on this and following rnds), 4 dc in same sc as joining; sk next 2 dc, sc in bl of next dc; * 5 dc in next sc; sk next 2 dc, sc in bl of next dc; rep from * 4 times more; join in 3rd ch of beg ch-3.

Rnd 4: Sl st in next 2 dc; ch 1, sc in same dc as last sl st made; sk next 2 dc, 7 dc in next sc; * sk next 2 dc, sc in next dc, sk next 2 dc, 7 dc in next sc; rep from * 4 times more; join in first sc: six 7-dc groups.

Rnd 5: Ch 1, sc in same sc as joining; * sc in next dc, hdc in next dc, dc in next dc, 3 dc in next dc; dc in next dc, hdc in next dc, sc in next dc, sc in next sc; rep from * 5 times more, ending last rep without working last sc; join in first sc: 60 sts.

Rnd 6: Ch 1, sc in same sc as joining; * sk next sc, hdc in next hdc, dc in next dc, 3 dc in each of next 3 dc; dc in next dc, hdc in next dc, sc in next 2 sc; rep from * 5 times more, ending last rep without working last sc; join in first sc: 90 sts.

Rnd 7: Ch 1, sc in same sc as joining; * sc in next hdc, hdc

Ruffled Heart   Sunshine and Ruffles

in next 2 sts, dc in next 2 dc, 3 dc in each of next 3 dc; dc in next 2 dc, hdc in next 2 sts, sc in next 3 sc; rep from * 5 times more, ending last rep without working last sc; join in first sc: 126 sts. Join yellow by drawing lp through; cut white.

Rnd 8: Sl st in next sc; ch 3 (counts as a dc), dc in next 7 sts, 2 dc in each of next 3 dc; dc in next 8 sts, sk next 2 sc, * dc in next 8 sts, 2 dc in each of next 3 dc; dc in next 8 sts, sk next 2 sc; rep from * 4 times more; join in 3rd ch of beg ch-3. Finish off and weave in all ends.

Back

With yellow, ch 6; join to form a ring.

Rnds 1 through 8: Rep Rnds 1 through 8 of Front. At end of Rnd 8, do not finish off; weave in short ends.

Edging and Hanging Loop:

Hold Front and Back with wrong sides tog; carefully matching sts, sl st in bl of corresponding dc of Front, joining Front and Back tog.

Rnd 1: * Ch 5, working through both sides, sc in bls of next dc; rep from * around; sc in sp between last sc made and next sc; ch 12, sl st in same sp; ch 1, sc in each ch, sl st in same sp as last sl st made. Finish off and weave in ends.

5: Ruffled Heart

Size:

About 10" at widest point before edging

Materials:

Worsted weight yarn,
   2 oz (140 yds) green;
   50 yds white
Size G aluminum crochet hook, or size required for gauge

Gauge:

4 hdc = 1"

Instructions

Front/Back (make 2)

With green, ch 2.

Row 1 (right side): 3 sc in 2nd ch from hook; ch 1, turn.

Row 2: 2 sc in first sc; sc in next sc, 2 sc in next sc: 5 sc; ch 2 (counts as first hdc on following rows), turn.

Row 3: Hdc in first sc; hdc in next 3 sc; 2 hdc in next sc: 7 hdc; ch 2, turn.

Row 4: Hdc in first hdc, hdc in each hdc to last hdc; 2 hdc in next hdc; ch 2, turn.

Rows 5 through 17: Rep Row 4. At end of Row 17: 35 hdc.

Left Side:

Row 18: Hdc in first hdc, hdc in next 16 hdc: 18 hdc; ch 2, turn, leaving rem hdc unworked.

Row 19: Dec over next 2 hdc [to work dec: (YO, draw up lp in next hdc) twice; YO and draw through all 5 lps on hook: dec made]; hdc in next 14 hdc, 2 hdc in next hdc: 18 hdc; ch 2, turn.

Row 20: Hdc in each hdc; ch 2, turn.

Row 21: Dec; hdc in next 13 hdc, dec: 16 hdc; ch 2, turn.

Row 22: Hdc in next 13 hdc, dec: 15 hdc; ch 2, turn.

Row 23: Dec; hdc in each hdc: 14 hdc; ch 2, turn.

Row 24: Dec; hdc in next 9 hdc, dec: 12 hdc; ch 2, turn.

Row 25: Dec; hdc in next 7 hdc, dec: 10 hdc; ch 2, turn.

Row 26: Hdc in next 7 hdc; dec: 9 hdc. Finish off.

Right Side:

Hold potholder with wrong side facing you; join green in 2nd unworked hdc of Row 17 from left side.

Row 1: Ch 2 (counts as an hdc), hdc in next 15 hdc; 2 hdc in next hdc: 18 hdc; ch 2, turn.

Row 2: Hdc in first hdc, hdc in next 15 hdc, dec: 18 hdc; ch 2, turn.

Row 3: Hdc in each hdc; ch 2, turn.

Row 4: Dec; hdc in next 13 hdc, dec: 16 hdc; ch 2, turn.

Row 5: Dec; hdc in next 13 hdc: 15 hdc; ch 2, turn.

Row 6: Hdc in next 12 hdc; dec: 14 hdc; ch 2, turn.

Row 7: Dec; hdc in next 9 hdc, dec: 12 hdc; ch 2, turn.

Row 8: Dec; hdc in next 7 hdc, dec: 10 hdc; ch 2, turn.

Row 9: Dec; hdc in next 7 hdc; continuing around heart, sc in side of each row and in each st around and working 3 sc in unused lp of beg ch; join in first sc. Finish off and weave in ends.

Edging:

Hold Front and Back with wrong sides tog; carefully matching stitches and working in bls of both sides, join white in first sc at center top of heart.

Rnd 1: Ch 2 (counts as an hdc), working in bls of both sides, hdc in next 8 hdc, 2 hdc in next hdc; (hdc in next 9 hdc, 2 hdc in next hdc) twice; hdc in next 16 hdc, 3 hdc in next hdc; hdc in next 16 hdc, (2 hdc in next hdc, hdc in next 8 hdc) twice; 2 hdc in next hdc; hdc in next 8 hdc: 98 hdc; join in 2nd ch of beg ch-2.

Rnd 2: Ch 1, sc in same ch as joining and in next 2 hdc; † hdc in next hdc, 3 dc in next hdc; hdc in next hdc, sc in next hdc †; rep from † to † 10 times more; hdc in next hdc, 3 dc in next hdc; dc in next hdc, 3 hdc in next hdc; sc in next hdc; rep from † to † 11 times; sc in next 2 hdc; join in first sc. Do not finish off.

Hanger:

Ch 14, sl st in same sc as joining; ch 1, sc in each ch; sl st in same sc as joining. Finish off and weave in all ends.

6: Mile-A-Minute Afghan

Size:
About 42" x 66"

Materials:
Worsted weight yarn,
  19 oz (1330 yds) off white;
  16 oz (1120 yds) raspberry
Size H aluminum crochet hook, or size required for gauge

Gauge:
7 dc = 2"
2 dc rows = 1"

Instructions

Panel (make 8)

Center Strip:
With off white, ch 14.

Row 1 (right side): Dc in 4th ch from hook (3 skipped chs count as a dc), ch 2, sk next 3 chs, 3 dc in next ch; ch 1, dc in next ch, ch 2, sk next 3 chs, dc in next 2 chs; ch 3 (counts as first dc on following rows), turn.

Row 2: Dc in next dc, ch 2, sk next ch-2 sp and next dc, in next ch-1 sp work (3 dc, ch 1, dc), ch 2, sk next 3 dc and next ch-2 sp, dc in next 2 dc; ch 3, turn.

Rows 3 through 99: Rep Row 2. At end of Row 99, do not ch 3. Finish off and weave in ends.

Strip Border:
Note: Border is worked around center strip.

Hold center strip with right side facing you and one long edge at top; join raspberry in first sp in upper right-hand corner.

Note: Dc on long sides are worked into sps formed by edge dc.

Rnd 1: Ch 3 (counts as a dc on this and following rnds), in same sp work (dc, ch 2, 2 dc): corner made; † ch 2, sk next sp, in next sp work (dc, ch 1, dc): V-st made †; rep from † to † 47 times more; ch 2, sk next sp, in next sp work (2 dc, ch 2, 2 dc): corner made; ch 2, sk next lp, sk next dc, between

next 2 dc work (dc, ch 1, dc): V-st made; ch 2, sk next lp, in next sp on long edge work (2 dc, ch 2, 2 dc): corner made; rep from † to † 48 times; ch 2, sk next sp, in next sp work (2 dc, ch 2, 2 dc): corner made; ch 2, sk next lp, between 2nd and 3rd dc of next 4-dc group work (dc, ch 1, dc): V-st made; ch 2; join in 3rd ch of beg ch-3.

Rnd 2: Sl st in next dc and in next ch-2 sp; ch 3, in same sp work (dc, ch 2, 2 dc): corner made; † ch 5, sc in ch-1 sp of next V-st †; rep from † to † 47 times more; ch 5, in ch-2 sp of next corner work (2 dc, ch 2, 2 dc): corner made; rep from † to † once; ch 5, in ch-2 sp of next corner work (2 dc, ch 2, 2 dc): corner made; rep from † to † 48 times; ch 5, in ch-2 sp of next corner work (2 dc, ch 2, 2 dc): corner made; rep from † to † once; ch 5; join in 3rd ch of beg ch-3.

Rnd 3: Sl st in next dc and in next ch-2 sp; ch 3, in same sp work (2 dc, ch 2, 3 dc): corner made; † ch 1, sc in next ch-5 lp, ch 1, 3 dc in next sc †; rep from † to † 47 times more; ch 1, sc in next ch-5 lp, ch 1, in ch-2 sp of next corner work (3 dc, ch 2, 3 dc): corner made; ch 1, sc in next ch-5 lp, ch 1, in next sc work (dc, ch 1, dc, ch 1, dc); ch 1, sc in next ch-5 lp, ch 1, in ch-2 sp of next corner work (3 dc, ch 2, 3 dc): corner made; rep from † to † 48 times; ch 1, sc in next ch-5 lp, ch 1, in ch-2 sp of next corner work (3 dc, ch 2, 3 dc): corner made; ch 1, sc in next ch-5 lp, ch 1, in next sc work (dc, ch 1, dc, ch 1, dc); ch 1, sc in next ch-5 lp, ch 1; join in 3rd ch of beg ch-3. Finish off and weave in ends.

Assembling

Hold two Panels with center strip sts in the same direction, wrong sides together and long edges at top; join off white in upper right-hand corner ch-2 sp; ch 1, sc in same sp as joining; working in bls only of both Panels, sc in each st along side. Finish off and weave in ends.

Rep with rem Panels.

Border

Note: Border is worked around entire afghan.

Hold afghan with right side facing you; join off white in ch-2 sp of upper right-hand corner; ch 1, 3 sc in same sp as joining; sc in each st and each ch-1 sp around and working 3 sc in each rem outer corner ch-2 sp; join in first sc. Finish off and weave in ends.

7: Baby Afghan and Hat/Bonnet

Size:
Afghan - about 33" x 41"
Hat/Bonnet- to 3 months

Materials:
Sport weight yarn, 14 oz (1540 yds) white; 3 oz (330 yds) each pink, lt blue, mint green, lavender, and lt yellow
Size E aluminum crochet hook, or size required for gauge

Gauge:
Motif = 2 3/4" x 2 3/4"

Instructions

Afghan
Motif (make 180)
Note: Motifs are made using pastel colors for Rnds 1 and 2 and using white for Rnd 3.

With any pastel color, ch 4; join to form a ring.

Rnd 1 (right side): Ch 3 (counts as a dc on this and following rnds), 2 dc in ring; (ch 2, 3 dc in ring) 3 times; ch 2; join in 3rd ch of beg ch-3. Finish off.

Rnd 2: Join any second pastel in any ch-2 sp; ch 3, in same sp work (2 dc, ch 2, 3 dc): beg corner made; * ch 1, sk next 3 dc, in next ch-2 sp work (3 dc, ch 2, 3 dc): corner made; rep from * twice more; ch 1, sk next 3 dc; join in 3rd ch of beg ch-3. Finish off.

Rnd 3: Join white in any corner ch-2 sp; ch 3, in same sp as joining work (2 dc, ch 2, 3 dc): beg corner made; * ch 1, sk next 3 dc, 3 dc in next ch-1 sp, ch 1, sk next 3 dc, in next corner ch-2 sp work (3 dc, ch 2, 3 dc): corner made; rep from * twice more; ch 1, sk next 3 dc, 3 dc in next ch-1 sp, ch 1, sk next 3 dc; join in 3rd ch of beg ch-3. Finish off.

Assembling
Join motifs in 15 rows of 12 motifs. To join motifs, hold 2 motifs with right sides tog. Carefully matching sts on both motifs and with white, sew with overcast st in bls only (see page 21) across side, beg and ending with one corner st. Join squares in rows; then sew rows tog in same manner, being sure that all four-corner junctions are firmly joined.

Edging
With right side of afghan facing you and short end at top, join white in ch-2 sp of upper right-hand corner.

Rnd 1: Ch 1, 5 sc in same sp as joining: corner made; * † sc in each st across motif to last st before joining; hdc in next st, dc in joining, hdc in next st on next motif †; rep from † to † across to last motif; sc in each st across last motif to corner ch-2 sp; 5 sc in corner ch-2 sp: corner made; rep from * 3 times more, ending last rep without working last corner; join in first sc.